MUSKOKA DINING GUIDE
& FAVOURITE RECIPES

MUSKOKA
Dining Guide & Favourite Recipes

NATURAL HERITAGE / NATURAL HISTORY INC.

Canadian Cataloguing in Publication Data

Main entry under title:

Muskoka dining guide and favourite recipes

Includes index.
ISBN 0-920474-77-2

1. Restaurants, lunch rooms, etc. - Ontario - Muskoka - Guidebooks. 2. Cookery - Ontario - Muskoka. 3. Muskoka (Ont.) - Description and travel - Guidebooks. I. Pare, Alice, 1942-

TX907.5C32M88 1992   647.95713'16   C92-094688-7

ACKNOWLEDGEMENTS
Almaguin Highlands Chamber of Commerce, Haliburton Highlands Chamber of Commerce, Huntsville/Lake of Bays Chamber of Commerce

COVER PHOTOGRAPHS
Inside front cover: *Victoria Hotel, Honey Harbour, 1910*
Inside back cover: *The Steamer Iroquois at Grove Park Lodge Wharf, circa 1940.*

PHOTOGRAPHIC CREDITS
Muskoka Pioneer Museum, The Ross Boothby Collection, Dr. N. Hunt (front cover)

SOURCES FOR INTRODUCTION
Boyer, Barbara: *Muskoka's Grand Hotels,* (The Boston Mills Press) 1987
Braithwaite, Max: *Max Braithwaite's Ontario* (J.J. Douglas Ltd.) 1974
Northway, Mary L.: *Nominigan: A casual history* (privately published) 1969
Northway, Mary L.: *Nominigan: The early years* (privately published) 1970
Big things happening at Bigwin this year. The Muskoka Sun (Susan Pryke, staff writer) Sept. 12, 1991.

DESIGN: Glen Patchet and Brian Williams (cover)

Printed and bound in Canada by Hignell Printing Limited

PREFACE

We have been asked many times what inspired us to publish a dining guide. This book came into being as a result of our own search for dining opportunities in the Muskoka area. Word of mouth and chance discoveries as we drove around the countryside have provided us with some wonderful dining experiences. It occurred to us that a dining guide which includes a choice atmosphere from rustic to sophisticated and a choice of cuisine from homestyle to gourmet would be appreciated by visitors, cottagers and residents alike.

The *Muskoka Dining Guide and Favourite Recipes* also offers a nostalgic glimpse of the early days including archival photographs, and some exciting recipes.

Although this book is entitled *Muskoka Dining Guide and Favourite Recipes*, we have expanded the scope to include the surrounding areas of Algonquin Park, Haliburton, East Parry Sound and Parry Sound. We hope that the readers who enjoy exploring throughout "cottage country" will find this helpful.

In the interest of maintaining uniformity of format and content, editorial discretion has been exercised in the organization of Areas 1, 2, 3 and 4. The information key at the bottom of the left-hand pages is provided for your convenience. We recommend that you call individual establishments if you have more specific requirements.

For detailed information regarding attractions and events, please call the Tourist Information and Chamber of Commerce for each area.

We invite you to visit the establishments presented in this book and enjoy the legendary "cottage country" cuisine.

Beverley Patchet
Paul Patchet
Jim Van Patten
Loraine Pare

LAKE OF BAYS PUBLICATIONS

CONTENTS

THE MAGIC OF MUSKOKA

～❦～

Muskoka, the very name itself evokes the imagery of sun-speckled summers and relaxed holidayers basking in the luxury of sumptuous resorts. Muskoka, a haven from the oppressive heat of the more southerly cities, has lured hundreds of families to the gingerbread verandahs and elegant diningrooms of the hotels nestled among the rugged granite outcroppings and the towering forests. The magic of Muskoka with its clean fragrant air and sparkling waters led to the glory days of the steamboats. Equipped with promenade decks, panelled lounges and dining

The WaWa Hotel, Lake of Bays, circa 1910.

-ix-

salons, these steamers shared the lakes with supply boats laden with delicacies for the hotels, people paddling for pleasure and regular freight steamers. During the period from the late 1800's to the early days of the twentieth century, Musk-oka was to emerge as one of the major vacation centres of Cana-da.

Today tourism remains as the most important industry for the area. Throughout one can still find reminders of this opulent heritage from a gentler time coexisting with the more modern, luxurious versions of resort hotels geared for the twenty-first century.

Muskoka wasn't always a holiday haven. Almost a century was to pass from the time Governor Simcoe arrived in 1791 to represent the British Crown in York (Toronto), with the subsequent settling of southern Ontario, before people even heard of Muskoka. Other than Ojibway hunters and the occasional intrepid fisherman, it was lumbermen in search of fresh stands of tall timbers, especially the pine, that gradually opened the way. In the 1850's the Muskoka Road was the first major artery to be chopped through the woods. But even then the well-to-do of the time, seeking respite from their urban setting, found their summer relaxation along the shores of Lake Ontario, Lake Erie and the mighty St. Lawrence. The mere thought of venturing north through unknown territory fraught with the horrors of wild animals, mosquitoes and black flies would have been considered ludicrous.

It took two adventurous young men from Toronto, John Campbell and James Bain, to initiate the notion of a summer holiday in the Free Grant lands of Muskoka in 1860. To reach their destination they took a train to Lake Simcoe, a steamboat to Orillia and a rowboat to the Severn Bridge area where they stayed overnight in a rustic log tavern. The remainder of the journey was on foot along the recent rough-hewn Muskoka Road to the shores of Muskoka Bay, the future site of Gravenhurst.

By 1864 they, along with some hardy friends including a few daring women, had formed the Muskoka Club. Yoho Island on Lake Joseph became the site for their clubhouse. By the end of the 1860's jerry-built hotels were springing into place for fearless travellers, workmen and landseekers around the future sites of Gravenhurst and Bracebridge. More construction was underway, including a canal lock to join Lake Rousseau to Lake Muskoka.

The man responsible for this shipping lock, being built to open the Muskoka Lakes for navigation, was Alexander Peter Cockburn. The son of successful Scottish immigrants who had originally settled in Stormont County, he was known as an industrious astute entrepreneur. Cockburn had recognized the potential of Muskoka as a tourist development bonanza. Following an exploratory tour of the area, he prepared an enthusiastic report for the Honourable Thomas D'Arcy McGee. Once government support was assured, he leased his existing enterprise and began construction of an emporium in Gravenhurst. Within a few years he was operating six

Empress Victoria, 1894-1915

stagecoaches to handle the influx of immigrants and freight and had several steamers and tugs working the Muskoka waters. His constant urging led to railway expansion from Orillia. In August 1875 a jubilant crowd welcomed the first steam locomotive to Gravenhurst and, by November of that, year an extended track permitted the grand opening of the new Muskoka Wharf Station.

With access to Muskoka now in place, tourist promotion could begin in earnest. Cockburn, by then a member of Parliament and an avowed champion of the North, was spending much of his winters preparing advertising literature and touring major American cities as a spokesman for the Muskokas. True to style, he left no stone unturned. Media personnal and prominent politicians were wined and dined for free aboard his best steamers. By 1896, tourists, many from the United States, were pouring into Muskoka for the summer.

Americans were to play a major role in building resort hotels to entice the holidayers. Many became builders of cottages to house those who chose to acquire land and become temporary Muskoka residents. In fact, the first wilderness grand hotel in Canada was established in Muskoka by a somewhat eccentric, but imaginative and wealthy American from New York. William H. Pratt's three-story building, the Rousseau House, opened to guests in July, 1870. For thirteen years this elegant, spacious mansion brought thousands of guests, both as individuals and as families. They came from as far away as the Southern United States and England despite the arduous journey required of the travellers in order to reach their destination. Without warning disaster struck. One bright October morning in 1883, fire entirely demolished the intricate frame structure and its contents. Only the chimneys remained. Fortunately the few autumn guests escaped unharmed. Although the hotel was never rebuilt, the recognition of wilderness hotels as successful enterprises was firmly established.

With the loss of Pratt's establishment, another frame structure, the Summit House, sprang into prominence. Built in the early 1870's by Hamilton Fraser, a merchant from Brampton and a friend of A.P. Cockburn, on a point overlooking Lake Joseph at Port Cockburn, the three-story building had been designed to cater to sportsmen and landseekers. By the 1890's it was the largest family-oriented resort in the Muskokas. With a Ditchburn boat livery established next door, a church for Sunday worship, acetylene lighting and a golf course, it was known as a first-class hotel. Unfortunately the Summit House also became the victim of an autumn fire in 1915. Fortunately no lives were lost, but once again the total destruction and the reality of inadequate insurance meant no re-building. Port Cockburn became a ghost town.

The depression of 1873 and the accompanying hard times curtailed the growth of tourism, but with the coming of the 1880's a new breed of tourist hosts brought renewed energy and enthusiasm to Muskoka. These were the farmers turned hotel operators. Their introductions to the unproductive thin, stony soil with short growing seasons followed by oppressive winters had caused them to rethink their futures. Experience with city folk seeking good fishing spots, a spot to stay and, most importantly, a place to spend ready money, led to the gradual evolution of some local farm homes from summer

Huntsville Station, 1900.

boarding house to resort inn. By the 1890's this transformation had spread from the Lake Rousseau -Lake Joseph area through the Lake Muskoka region and into the Huntsville, Lake of Bays country. With lumbering in decline and agriculture a questionable pursuit, tourism was viewed as the alternative source of employment and income for Muskoka in the rapidly approaching twentieth century.

The stories, myths and fireside tales of the grand old hotels are legendary as indeed are the splendid structures that once embellished the shores of the lakes. Although far too numerous to recount in detail here, one would be amiss in not highlighting a few of the more remarkable that are no longer with us but, very much part of the Muskoka heritage.

LAKE ROSSEAU-LAKE JOSEPH

The Royal Muskoka Hotel developed by a Toronto lawyer, E.L. Sawyer and designed by Lucius Bloomer, the architect who later would build the Waldorf Astoria in New York, became known as 'the Grand Old Dame of the Lake.' Built on Lake Rousseau in 1901 on 130 acres at a cost of about $150,000.00, the hotel could accommodate 350 guests by 1902, in the most luxurious of settings. With electric lighting, hot and cold running water plus a full range of recreation and social activities, the Royal Muskoka provided luxury holidays to an impressive list of dignitaries during its heyday. In fact the impressive steamship, the Sagamo, flagship of the Muskoka Lake Navigation Company, was launched in 1906 to help handle the great crowds flocking to the hotel. With the Depression followed by World War I, the good times seemed over. Despite efforts to revive the grand dame in the late forties, the results were disappointing. On May 18, 1952, the hotel disappeared in an all consuming blaze. Today history buffs can find a handful of small treasures snatched from the smouldering debris housed at the Port Carling Pioneer Museum.

Bigwin Inn, Lake of Bays, c. 1920.

HUNTSVILLE, LAKE OF BAYS

Off the shore of Norway Point in the Lake of Bays is Bigwin Island, named after Joseph Bigwin, a First Nations chief of the Algonquins who once camped and trapped throughout the area. In 1893, following the logging out of the 620 acre island, Reuben Millichamp of Toronto bought the property from the Ontario government for $1.00 per acre. By 1912, Charles Orland Shaw of Huntsville, had acquired the picturesque island and had begun construction of his vision, the biggest and classiest summer resort in Ontario. C.O. Shaw, owner of the Anglo-Canadian Leather Company, was a flamboyant industrialist with a penchant for the best that money could buy. Himself musically inclined, he encouraged and accommodated the musical interests of his primarily Italian workforce, gradually creating the finest concert band in North American, the Anglo-Canadian Concert Band. Using his international connections, he would lure some of the most exceptional dance band musicians, even from the celebrated Paul

Whiteman's Orchestra, to come and play in Hunts-ville and later in his Bigwin Inn. Construction of this hotel was halted during World War I, but resumed in haste following the Armstice to bring about the formal opening in June 1920. With 280 rooms, space enough for 700 guests, an enormous twelve-sided dining room and a dance pavilion overlooking the water, the elegant Bigwin was host to millionaires seeking an exclusive holiday setting. The formal dinners and afternoon teas in ex-quisite surroundings were served by immaculate and discreet waiters and waitresses. An oft told story tells of the film stars Clark Gable and Carole Lombard there for a romantic interlude and Princess Juliana of the Netherlands with bodyguards there as a guest of the Canadian government during World War II. Travel agents for the rich and famous in the United States competed for the exclusive right to book the Bigwin.. But times were about to change. The exceptional success of the twenties was shattered by the Depression of the thirties. Even the mini boom during war-time, with Europe a war zone and the Caribbean not yet popular, failed to last. A newer crowd was seeking a different type of resort holiday with liquor available, a racier environment acces-sible by car and more informal excitement. Following C.O. Shaw's death in 1942, the Bigwin never regained its former greatness, despite efforts of succeeding owners to modernize and update. By 1969, Bigwin was acquired by Bigisle Enterprised Ltd. with the intention of turning it into condominiums. Today there are only a few condos in use, but the grander ideas still per-sist waiting for better times. Today, Bigwin itself stands empty, its crumbling buildings a forlorn reminder of the finest international resort Ontario could offer.

NORTH MUSKOKA

Limberlost Lodge, named from the series of books writ-ten by Gene Stratton-Porter in the early twentieth century, was established in 1921. This more northerly resort was famous for its cosy, rustic wilderness environment. Located deep in the

Limberlost Lodge, c. 1940.

forest it had splendid access for camp-outs to nearby smaller spring-fed lakes. Unlike the majority of resorts of the time, this was a year round business. Summer featured horseback riding with miles of forest trails and overnight camp-outs. Winter provided downhill skiing. By the late 1930's the hill known as "Top of the World" was developed, complete with a ski tow in place. Clearly this was the resort for the out-of-doors enthusiast, the naturalist, and the more recreationally-minded seeking an active holiday rather than the leisurely pampering of the summer only sites. Demolished by fire in 1942, Limberlost was rebuilt, but this time with only one storey. With the passing of the owner, Gordon Hill in the late forties, the lodge no longer had a proprietor fulfilling a dream. In 1985 Limberlost was torn down.

ALGONQUIN PARK

Another wilderness site, Nominigan, located in Algonquin Park, is again a story of a fabled resort doomed to an unseemly end, this time as a dismembered pile of hand-hewn logs. With the opening of the railway from Ottawa to Parry Sound in 1895, city dwellers now had easier access to the wilderness. The Highland Inn, a railway hotel built in 1905 near the Park Station and close to the railway, began as headquarters for fisherman and campers. Soon it could no longer satisfy the guests seeking a more wilderness experience, but one with some of the rudiments of luxury such as hot and cold running water, lighting and good meals. This need led to the Nominigan. Built in 1913 on a point in Smoke Lake among the balsams, the hotel was the vacation outpost of the Grand Trunk and later the Canadian National Railways. The white cedar log lodge with its six guest houses was to become a favourite for fisherman and nature lovers with their families. Despite the seven mile bush trip by stage or the paddle and portage entry from Highland Inn, Nominigan usually ran the season at its capacity of nearly a hundred people. Often entire families including grandparents would stay for one or two months. Year after year the same families would visit, some from as far away as England.

Tom Thomson, originally from Owen Sound, was well known at Nominigan both as a budding artist and as a part-time guide. It is believed that it was at Nominigan that he met Lawren Harris, a senior member of the Group of Seven, who was a regular at the resort.

In 1928, a fire destroyed the six cabins, but fortunately because of the wind direction, the Lodge and Guide House were spared. For three years the buildings remained vacant except for some occasional renting to fishing parties. In 1931 Garfield Northway, owner of the Northway Department Stores and a frequent guest from his childhood days acquired the property. For a number of years, the newly landscaped and repaired Nominigan was the setting for family and hordes of guests over the summer months.

A change in Park Policy in the 1940's stipulated that property would revert to the government once the lease had expired. After Garfield's death in 1960, with fifteen years left on

The Albion Hotel dining room, Gravenhurst, c. 1920.

the lease, Dr. Harry and Adele Ebbs maintained the property, both for personal use and some times as a camp site for students and their instructors. In 1975 according to the policy, Nominigan and its outbuildings were to be destroyed by fire. With some negotiation, Dr. Ebbs managed to have the magnificent logs dismantled from the lodge before the area was torched. Today nothing remains of the much loved Nominigan.

Sumptuous meals with emphasis on quality and service were a feature of the grand old hotels. Gleaming china with sparkling silver on starched tablecloths served by uniformed staff were the rigour of the major sites. Acquiring and maintaining fresh food, expecially meat and produce, was a major feat. In the days before refrigeration ice-boxes with sawdust were part of every establishment. The supply cars from Toronto stocked with staple foods and delicacies would leave Union Station to be met by steamer supply boats, "floatings stores", carrying their indispensible goods to the awaiting hotels and cottagers.

Today exceptional meals and special dishes remain a key feature of enjoyment and discussion for guests and tourists in the Muskoka area. Gone are the challenges of preservation and delivery, but the appetite whetted by the outdoor air remains. The following pages present for your enjoyment an invitation to sample the best from the kitchens of our selected establishments. Try them and experience a treat. Better still, come and visit in person. Participate in the magic of Muskoka.

J. Elizabeth Bruce
May, 1992

MUSKOKA DINING GUIDE
& FAVOURITE RECIPES

Area 1
South Muskoka, Parry Sound

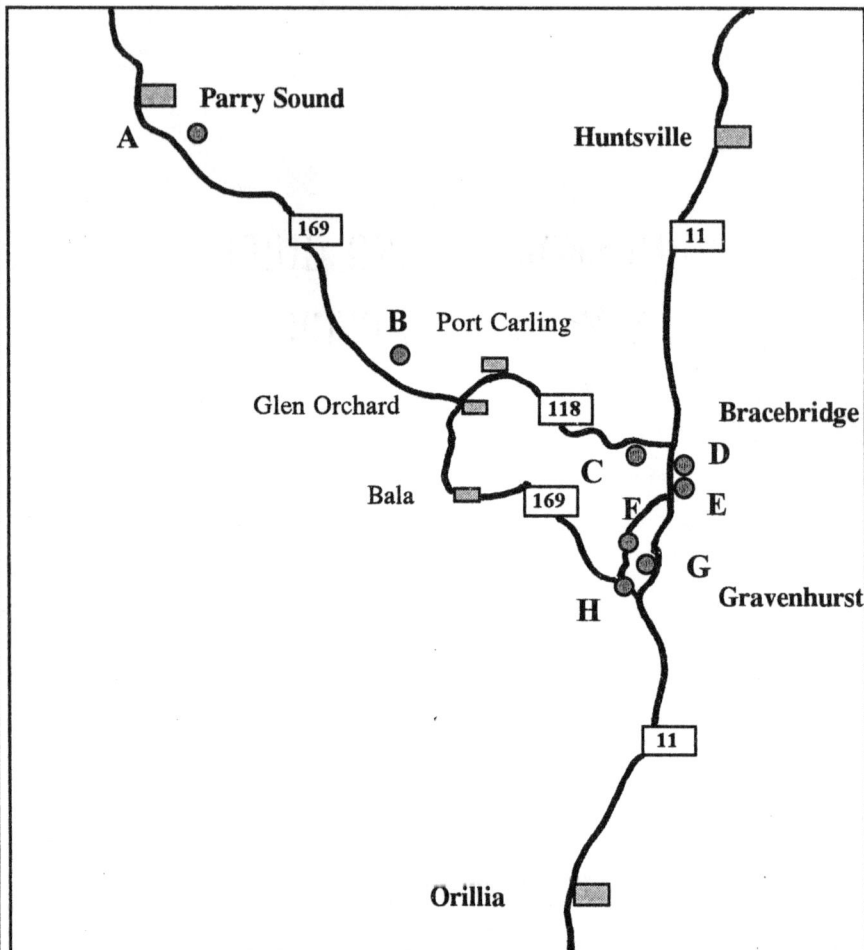

Parry Sound

A

Huntsville

169

11

B Port Carling

Glen Orchard

118

Bracebridge

C

D

Bala

169

E

F

G

H

Gravenhurst

11

Orillia

Index

A- Burton's Fine Dining
B- Sherwood Inn
C- Patterson-Kaye Lodge
D- The Old Station Restaurant
E- Inn at the Falls
F- Muskoka Sands Resort
G- Sloan's Restaurant
H- R.M.S. Segwun

Wigwassan Lodge, Lake Rosseau, c. 1950.

General Information

Waterways: Lake Muskoka, Lake Joseph, Lake Rosseau, Parry Sound

Major Centres: Bala, Bracebridge, Gravenhurst, Port Carling, Parry Sound

Cultural Attractions: South Muskoka: Bethune Memorial House, Muskoka Festival Theatre, Muskoka Lake Museum, Opera House Parry Sound: Festival of Sound, Rainbow Theatre

BURTON'S Fine Dining
RR 2, Parry Sound
Ont., P2A 2W8
(705) 746-7122

Your hosts: Kathy, Jim & Connie Dalrymple
Chef: Doug Wellington

This is the place for elegant dining in a warm and friendly atmosphere with exceptional service at Parry Sound's original log cabin restaurant. Burton's is a family run operation where they endeavour to spoil their patrons at all times. The restaurant features a variety of continental cuisine, homemade bread and pastries of superb quality.

Reservations recommended
Season: year round
Type of cuisine: Continental
Licensed LLBO
Credit cards: Visa, AMEX, MC
Wheelchair access
Children's portions
Dress code: casual
Price range: $14-30

Garlic Roasted Chateaubriand
with Cognac Mustard Sauce

14-16 oz filet mignon
1 cup   demi glaze or Campbell's beef broth
3 tbsp   stone ground mustard
1 oz   cognac
3   large garlic buds

Roast filet and garlic to preferred taste at 425^0 F. Deglaze pan with cognac. Add demi glaze and bring to a boil. Add mustard. Simmer for 5 minutes. Slice filet and place on plate. Cover with sauce.

Serves 2

Sherwood Inn

P.O. Box 400, Port Carling, Ont.
P0B 1J0
(705) 765-3131
(800) 461-4233

General Manager: John K. Heineck

Winner of the prestigious AAA/CAA Four Diamond Award for Excellence, the Inn sits amongst towering pines on the shore of Lake Joseph. With its air of tranquility, Sherwood Inn provides an unrivalled combination of atmosphere, good service and gastronomic excellence, complimented by an extensive wine cellar. Service is at the heart of Sherwood Inn - personal, efficient and unobtrusive 53 years in Muskoka.

Reservations required
Season: year round
Type of cuisine: "Modern Country House"
Licensed LLBO
Credit cards: All major
No wheelchair access
Dress code: casual; Lounge & Dining Room after 6 pm require jackets (men)
Price range: Lunch from $6.50; 6 course Table d'hote dinner at $43 per person

Poached Pears Filled with Smoked Duck and Saffron Rice

4	medium sized, firm pears (any type)
2/3 cup	rice
1	smoked duck breast
1	small can Sweet Red pepper
1 cup	35% cream
1/2	lemon
2 tbsp	honey
	pinch of ginger
6	black peppercorns

Cook rice, with a pinch of saffron in water. Cool. Peel and core whole pears leaving the stem intact. Reserve peelings. Brush flesh with lemon juice to prevent discolouring.

Place pears, ginger, lemon juice, peppercorns and peelings in a pan, and cover with water. Poach over medium heat until soft (about 20 minutes).

Remove pears and allow to cool. Strain liquid. Add honey and reduce to a thick glaze. Hollow out pears with a melon baller and reserve pulp.

Finely dice one red pepper and puree remaining peppers in a blender with the pear pulp.

Finely dice the duck breast (removing fat), cook with pepper, rice and cream in frying pan until thick. Season with salt and pepper to taste.

Stuff the pears with mixture, cover pears with glaze and bake at 350⁰ F for 15 minutes. Pour 1 1/2 tbsp of the red pepper sauce onto the side of each plate. Cut each pear into four rings with a serrated knife, overlap rings opposite the sauce on each plate. Garnish with parsley.

Serves 4

Patterson-Kaye Lodge

RR 1, Bracebridge, Ont., POB 1C0
(705) 645-4169

Owners: Christine & Norman Miller
Chef: Cal Morrison

Patterson-Kaye, established in 1936, was purchased in 1959 by Ann and Frank Miller (a former Premier) and the Miller family continue to extend a warm welcome to their guests.

Nestled among the pines on Lake Muskoka near the mouth of the Muskoka River, the lodge offers a unique experience in an informal atmosphere. Our chef of 17 years takes pride in preparing excellent meals for individuals, families and groups.

Reservations recommended
Season: year round
Type of cuisine: Canadian
Not licensed
Credit cards: Visa, MC
No wheelchair access
Children's portions
Dress code: casual
Price range: $15-30

Patterson Kaye Seafood Linguini

1/4 cup	scallops
1/4 cup	baby clams
1/4 cup	crab meat
3 oz	fresh red salmon
1 cup	heavy cream
1/4 cup	butter
1/2 cup	sweet white wine
1 tbsp	concentrated fish stock
1 tbsp	brown sugar
1 clove	clove garlic
3	sprigs fresh tarragon
1/4 cup	cooking oil
1 tsp	salt
10 cups	water
1 lb	linguini
2 tbs	melted butter

In a deep fry pan melt butter and saute scallops, clams, crab meat and salmon. Add white wine and tarragon and simmer for 5 minutes. Add chopped garlic and fish stock. Add cream and sugar. Cook until mixture thickens (*if the mixture does not thicken enough, a little corn starch will help*). Reduce heat and stir occasionally.

Note: Fish stock concentrate can be quite salty. If you are using a powder substitute, salt may be needed according to taste.

In a sauce pan bring to a boil the oil, salt and water. Add linguini and cook 10-12 minutes or until soft. Strain linguini and put back in pot. Toss with melted butter. This will keep the linguini separate. Place linguini on individual plates and ladle on seafood sauce.

Serves 6-8

The Old Station Restaurant

88 Manitoba Street,
Bracebridge, Ont., P1L 1S1
(705) 645-9776

Owner/Manager Michael Warr
Chef: Robert Snelling

At the top of the hill on the main street of Bracebridge, dine under a 100 year old silver maple tree, which is the focal point of the dining room and one of the features that define the character of this unique restaurant.

Formerly a service station from 1934 to 1979, its rustic warmth, combined with the screened-in patio creates a year round dining experience for all.

Great food selection and service adds up to terrific times at the Old Station Restaurant.

Reservations accepted
Season: year round
Type of cuisine: Canadian/French
Licensed LLBO
Credit cards: Visa, AMEX, MC
No wheelchair access
Children's menu
Dress code: casual
Price range: $9-15

Chicken Fussili Primavera

10 oz   cooked rotini noodles
12 oz   blanched mixed vegetables (broccoli, cauliflower,
        zucchini, red peppers, carrots)
2-4 oz cooked boneless, skinless chicken breasts
1 cup   whipping cream
2 1/2 oz parmesan cheese
1 tsp   butter
2 tbsp dry white wine

    Over a medium heat mix together the cream, butter,
wine and parmesan cheese. Reduce heat and stir until the sauce
begins to thicken.
    Add the pre-cooked noodles, vegetables and thinly sliced
chicken, and toss together until all ingredients are combined.
    Serve on an oval plate and garnish with a slice of orange
and a pinch of nutmeg (optional).

Serves 2

Inn At The Falls

17 Dominion St.
Bracebridge, Ont., P1L 1R6
(705) 645-2245

Your Hosts: Jan and Peter Rickard
Chef: Dave Madsen

  Originally built in 1876, this fine old Victorian Inn exudes traditional old fashioned hospitality and charm. Located in a wooded, small town setting overlooking the Bracebridge Falls, this historic inn offers 20 well-appointed rooms, fireplaces, a heated outdoor pool, extensive English gardens and excellent food.
  "Victoria's" offers elegant, fine dining overlooking the Bracebridge Bay; the "Fox & Hounds" Pub and "The Patio" offer more casual fare.

Reservations not required
Season: open year round
Type of cuisine: European
Licensed LLBO
Credit cards: Visa, AMEX, MC
No wheelchair access
Dress code: casual
Price range: $4-12 (pub)
$12-25 (dining room)

Stuffed Sole Veronique

4	filets of sole
2 cups	crab meat
1 cup	baby shrimp
1 tsp	fresh dill
	freshly ground black pepper
2 cups	seedless green grapes
6 tbls	butter
1 cup	white wine
2 cups	35% cream

On a large pie plate place the sole in a cylindrical shape. Mix the crab and shrimp together and put in the middle of the sole. Sprinkle the crab and shrimp mixture with fresh dill and freshly ground pepper.

Bake in 350⁰ oven for 15 minutes. While sole is baking, take a saucepan and add butter, and when hot, add grapes and white wine. Reduce by half. Add cream and reduce by half until thickened. Add salt and pepper to taste.

Place sole on warm plate and cover with grape sauce.

Serves 4

MUSKOKA SANDS

Muskoka Beach Road,
Gravenhurst, Ont., P0C 1G0
(705) 687-2233

Manager: Lisa Whitely
Chef: Hubert Obermeier

Rediscover the Muskoka Sands Resort Hotel, a place rich in resort tradition, surrounded by splendid natural beauty and superb recreational facilities. This hotel has been renovated into one of the most spectacular resorts in Muskoka. Fine cuisine awaits in the elegant Winewood Dining Room. The gorgeous view of the lake and beyond are the perfect complement to any meal, whether it is breakfast, lunch or dinner. Whatever your pleasure, the Lobby Bar features an All Day Menu to enjoy in front of our fireplace or watching the sun set over the lake.

Muskoka Sands looks forward to welcoming you soon!

Reservations: recommended
Season: year round
Type of cuisine: Canadian/European
Licensed LLBO
Credit cards: Visa, AMEX, MC, En Route

Wheelchair access
Children's portions
Dress code: smart casual
(no jeans at dinner please!)
Price range: $25-35

Gratinated Fruit Dessert

A variety of fresh seasonal fruits
Sugar to taste
Kirsch liqueur
Juice of $1/2$ lemon
Juice of $1/2$ orange

Cream Sauce:
Grated rind of $1/3$ lemon
Grated rind of $1/3$ orange
3 $1/2$ oz butter
5 oz sugar
2 eggs
1 cup whipping cream

Cut up the fruit and place into a fireproof ceramic dish. Sprinkle with sugar and kirsch (cherry liqueur) to add fullness to the flavour of the fruit. Set aside.

Combine orange juice, lemon juice, rinds from lemon and orange and the butter and sugar. Warm all in a double boiler, and stir together. Crack the eggs and whip well.

Add to the eggs the warm ingredients and maintain heat until the mixture thickens. Set aside to cool. When cooled, fold in one cup of whipping cream.

Pour the finished orange-flavoured cream over the fruit. Place in oven under the broiler just until the cream browns slightly. It won't take long, so keep your eye on it!

Serves 6

Sloan's Restaurant & Tavern
155 Muskoka St. So.,
Gravenhurst, Ont., P0C 1G0
(705) 687-4611

Your hosts: Alan & Betty Tipple
Chef: Alan Tipple

For over 75 years, hungry travellers have devoured Sloan's famous wild blueberry pie. Relax in the Old Muskoka Room, built with hand hewn pine beams, or in the casual family restaurant. Be sure to try their milk shakes made the good old fashioned way. You'll feel right at home at this landmark in the heart of Gravenhurst.

Reservations recommended (summer only)
Season: year round
Type of cuisine: Canadian homestyle
Licensed LLBO
Credit cards: Visa, AMEX, MC
Wheelchair access (except washroom)
Children's portions
Dress code: casual
Price range: $12-15

Steak Neptune

4 oz	white vinegar
1 tsp	white pepper
1 tsp	tarragon leaves
1/4 tsp	parsley
8	egg yolks
3/4 lbs	butter
6-8 oz	beef tenderloins
24	pieces asparagus tips
6 oz	crab meat (cooked)
	Bernaise sauce

Combine vinegar, pepper, tarragon and parsley and simmer until almost dry. Cool slightly. Using a double boiler add egg yolks slowly, whipping well until thick. Remove from heat. Add butter slowly, whipping well.

Broil beef tenderloin to taste. Place 4 pieces asparagus, 1 oz crab meat and 3 oz Bernaise sauce on each piece of tenderloin. Broil 10 to 15 seconds and enjoy.

Serves 6

R.M.S. SEGWUN

The Royal Mail Ship Segwun
Sagamo Park, Hwy 169
Box 68, Gravenhurst, P0C 1G0
(705) 687-6667

Your Hosts: The Officers & Crew

    The **Royal Mail Ship Segwun** (which means springtime in Ojibway) has been sailing on the Muskoka Lakes since 1887. Originally, the Segwun carried supplies and passengers to the resorts and supplies and mail to the early settlers.

    In the 1990's the Segwun is being used by brides as a unique setting for weddings and many corporations use the ship for entertaining.

    Daily cruises from June 13 to Thanksgiving are available with lunch and dinner.

Reservations required
Season: see above
Type of cuisine: Canadian
Licensed LLBO
Credit cards: Visa, AMEX, MC
Wheelchair access
No children's portions
Dress code: casual
Price range: 3¹/₂ hour dinner cruises $42.50 (+ taxes)

1992 Sunset Dinner Cruise Menu

Freshly Baked Assorted Rolls

Glady's Garden Fresh Salad
with Segwun Dressing

Canadian Grade A Prime Rib of Beef
&
Chicken Cordon Bleu

Yes, you can have both as all the fresh Muskoka air
will increase your appetite!

Baby Glazed Carrots

Green Beans Almondine

Baked Potato

Choice of Dessert

Belgian Chocolate Mousse Cake
Blueberry Pie
Fresh Fruit Salad
Coffee or Tea

The Segwun has her own private labelled wines,
champagne, cognac and beer

plus, a 3¹/₂ hour cruise on Lake Muskoka

Area 2
North Muskoka, East Parry Sound

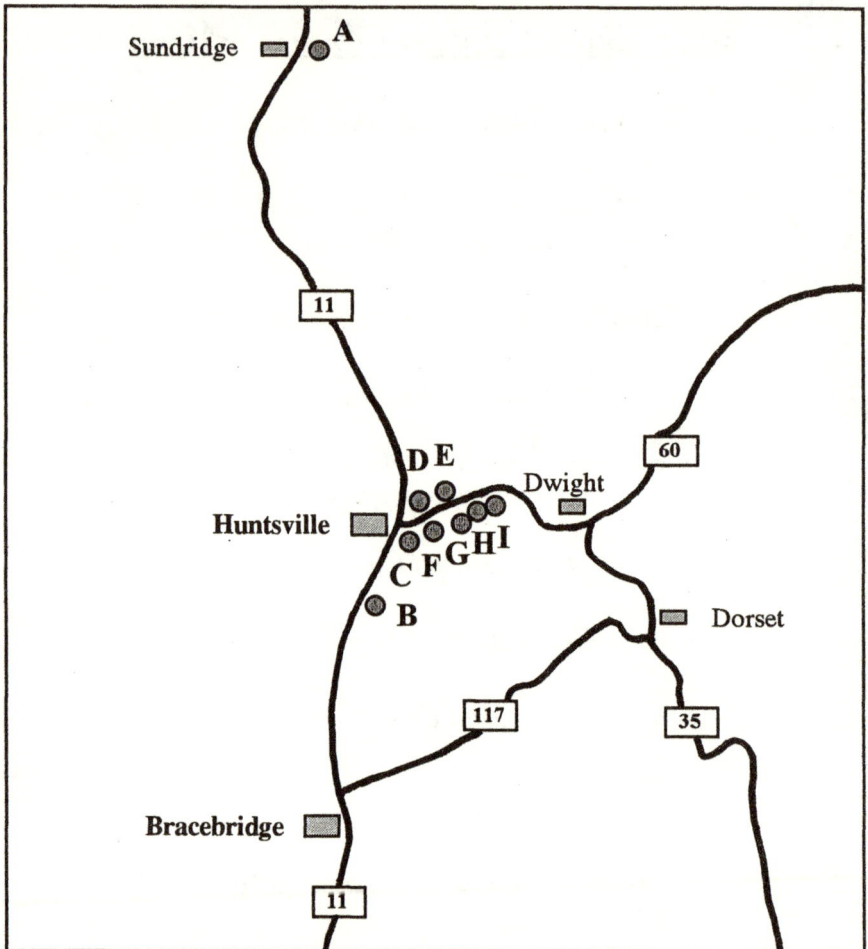

Sundridge ▪ ● **A**

11

D E

Huntsville ▪

C F G H I

B

Dwight ▪

60

▪ Dorset

117

35

Bracebridge ▪

11

Index

A- Northridge Inn
B- Gryffin Lodge
C- Muskoka Pioneer Village & Museum
D- Navigation Company Diner
E- Touch of Class
F- The Butcher's Daughters
G- Grandview Inn
H- Deerhurst Resort
I- Cedar Grove Lodge

The Canal Bridge, Huntsville, c. 1930.

General Information

Waterways: Mary Lake, Fairy Lake, Lake Vernon, Peninsula Lake, Lake Bernard

Major Centres: Burk's Falls, Huntsville, Port Sydney, Sundridge

Cultural Attractions: North Muskoka: Dyer Memorial Gardens, Muskoka Pioneer Village & Museum

East Parry Sound: Maple Sugar Houde & Museum, Blue Star Mine, Commanda General Store Museum

THE NORTH RIDGE INN

Northridge Inn
Box 87, Sundridge, Ont., P0A 1Z0
(705) 384-5373

Your host: Moe McGinty

For over 50 years disciminating couples have taken advantage of the private setting and casual hospitality offered on Lake Bernard's finest beach. Totally refurbished in 1989, the Inn is relaxed, well cared for and "wonderfully small". Canadiana, jazz, knotty pine and tartan. The Northridge Inn is all of these and more with fine cuisine, unparalleled scenery and personalized attention to your every need.

Reservations only
Season: year round
Type of cuisine: Canadian
Licensed LLBO
Credit cards: Visa, AMEX, MC
Wheelchair access
No children's portions
Dress code: smart casual
Price range: $25-35

Arctic Char Encroute

2-8 oz	char steaks (feather bones removed)
2 sheets	puff pastry 6" x 6"
	egg wash
20	fine chopped mushrooms
1	white onion (duxcelle)
6 oz	white wine
10 oz	35% cream
6 g	chopped chives

Egg wash the rolled puff pastry edges. Place 10 oz of duxcelle on center of each char steak. Place char in centre of puff pastry and fold each corner to the centre. Bake at 350° F until pastry is golden brown.

Sauce

Reduce white wine by half and add cream. Simmer to reduce by half. Add chives and season to taste. Pour sauce on plate and place char encroute on chive sauce.

Serves 2

Gryffin Lodge

Box 2308, Gryffin Lodge Road,
Huntsville, Ont., P0A 1K0
(705) 789-7491

Your hosts: William & Shelby van Stygeren
Chef: Larry Peck

In 1862, William Lawrence took advantage of a land grant and carved a 400 acre niche at the north shore of Mary's Lake. About 1895 the family built a two-storey mansard roof stone house.

Later, John and Mary Ostrofski, veterans of the Polish Free Forces during World War II extended the main house and added cabins in the surrounding woods. They named the property Gryffin Lodge from central-eastern European folklore.

In the 1970's the Hunter sisters updated the accomodation while maintaining the old Muskoka atmosphere and style.

Since 1987, this beautiful stone lodge has continued to flourish under the ownership of Bill and Shelby van Stygeren. The warm hospitality is exceeded only by the superb meals served in the cosy dining room overlooking a spectacular view. Gryffin Lodge welcomes you.

Reservations required
Season: year round
Type of cuisine: Canadian
Licensed LLBO
Credit cards: Visa, AMEX, MC

No wheelchair access
Children's portions
Dress code: casual
Price range: $15-20

Fettuccine Carbonara

1 tbsp	butter
4 oz	julienned prosciutto
2 oz	julienned bacon
2 oz	diced onion
1/2 cup	parmesan cheese
3	egg yolks
2 1/2 cups	whipping cream

Saute onion and bacon in butter for 4-5 minutes. Add the ham and cook for 2-3 minutes more. Add cream and bring to a boil for 7-8 minutes. Add freshly ground black pepper to taste and toss with fettuccine. Gradually add parmesan and toss. Quickly toss in egg yolk and remove from heat. Serve with garnish with parmesan cheese and freshly chopped parsley.

Serves 4-6

Zabaglione

6	egg yolks
2/3 cup	sweet Marsala wine
4 tbsp	dry white wine
2 tbsp	sugar

All ingredients must be at room temperature. Add ingredients into a stainless steel bowl, and place over a pot of boiling water. With a fine wire whisk, whisk until the zabaglione is light and slightly thickened. Be careful not to cook your egg mixture or it will scramble on you! Pour over fresh fruit or berries. Hot or cold.

Serves 4-6

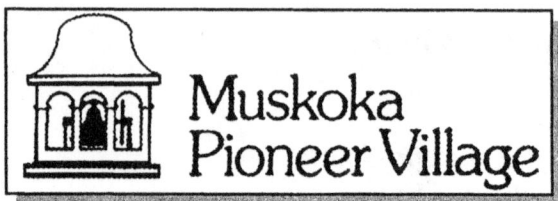

Muskoka Pioneer Village

Box 2802, Huntsville, Ont., P0A 1K0
(705) 789-7576

Director: John M. Finley

Muskoka Pioneer Village offers the visitor a unique opportunity to step back in time. The village has a collection of 17 early homesteads and buildings representing an active pioneer community as it existed between 1860 and 1910. Demonstrations of traditional pioneer crafts such as blacksmithing and candlemaking take place throughout the season.

While at the village, visitors have the opportunity to visit a fully operational general store, discover locally made gifts at Gramma's House, and experience rare pioneer dining. The Inn, overlooking their very own Cann Lake, features fares for all appetites plus tasty desserts.

Reservations recommended (for groups of 20 or more)
Season: year round
Type of cuisine: Early Canadian
Not Licensed
Credit cards: Visa, MC
No wheelchair access
Children's portions
Dress code: casual
Price range: $3-5 plus admisssion

Hot Spiced Wassail

Stud 3 oranges with whole cloves. In a pot, combine 6 cups apple juice or cider, 2 cups cranberry juice, 1/4 cup sugar plus 1 tsp aromatic bitters.

Add bag of spices plus oranges.

Simmer, covered, 10 minutes.

Stir in 1 cup rum and heat through.

Remove spices and oranges. Pour into a warm serving bowl and float oranges on top.

Serves many

THE NAVIGATION CO. DINER

The Navigation Co. Diner
Town Dock
Huntsville, Ont., P0A 1K0
(705) 789-7400

Manager: Jeff Suddaby & Ron Gostlin

During the 1940's and 50's the Huntsville Lake of Bays Navigation Co. provided transportation service for residents and tourists. 1988 saw the rebirth of this concept with the opening of the Navigation Co. Diner and Boat Tours at the site of the original Navigation Co. on Huntsville's Town Dock. The Lake of Bays rebirth occurred the following year with the "Depot" on Highway 60 Dwight.

Both restaurants provide imaginative fun, affordable menu's prepared by chefs that are always one step ahead of the competition and served by a staff second to none.

Reservations not needed
Season: year round
Type of cuisine: Canadian/Specialty
Licensed LLBO
Credit cards: Visa, AMEX, MC
No wheelchair access
Children's portions
Dress code: casual
Price range: $4-14

Chicken Fajitas

4-4 oz	chicken breasts
1 oz	vegetable oil
$1/2$	spanish onion (sliced)
2	green peppers (sliced)
1	red pepper (sliced)
$1/2$ cup	cut tomatoes
1 tsp	crushed chilis
4 oz	sour cream
4 oz	grated mozzarella
4 oz	salsa
4 oz	guacamole
4 oz	lime wedges
12	flour tortillas

In a frying pan, saute each chicken breast on low heat for approximately 5 minutes each side. Slice and place with vegetables. In a cast iron frying pan, place oil, green onions, green peppers and red peppers. Saute for 3 minutes on high heat, add chilis and tomatoes and let stand for 2 minutes. Serve in frying pan (make sure there is a hot pad on the table). Squeeze lime juice into mixture for flavour and sizzle.

Preheat flour tortillas in oven at 350^0 F for 5 minutes. Serve with salsa (of your choice), cheese, sour cream and guacamole.

Serves 4

TOUCH OF CLASS

Touch of Class (Boat Charters)
Huntsville, Ont., P0A 1K0
(705) 789-8980
(705) 789-6411 (Deerhurst)
(705) 789-7400 (Navigation Co.)

Your Hosts: Dan Patterson & Bev MacWilliams
Chef: Jeff Suddaby

     A unique dining experience on the beautiful Vernon, Peninsula, Fairy and Mary lakes is awaiting you and your friends. Choose a daily tour, a BBQ Riverboat Tour, or create your own tour with this service. Organize a Gourmet Dinner Cruise, a wedding cruise or a business meeting cruise. "Our only limit is your imagination!" Touch of Class can accomodate up to 8 people on the "Scout 30" and up to 15 on the luxury 28' Pontoon Boat.

Reservations on a first come basis
Season: May-October
Type of cuisine: your choice
Not Licensed
Credit cards: Visa, MC
Wheelchair access
Dress code: casual
Price range: $15 +

Touch of Class
Sample Menu

Lumache with Duck & Pistachio Nuts

Spinach Salad with Raspberry & Sweet Honey Vinaigrette

Filet Mignon & Shrimp with Crab

Fresh Vegetables

Rice & Peppers

Profiteroles

Tea or Coffee

THE BUTCHER'S DAUGHTERS
133 Hwy 60, Huntsville, Ont., P0A 1K0
(705) 789-2848

The Daughters (and Chefs) : Julia Bosch, Keely Schierl

This old world delicatessen offers imported specialties, cheeses and outstanding home-made fresh and smoked meats. It is an ideal spot for a quick lunch in a warm atmosphere.

Call or stop in for picnic lunches, homestyle catering, or party trays for all occasions.

Reservations not required
Season: year round
Type of cuisine: Canadian/European
Not licensed
Credit cards: Visa
No wheelchair access
Children's portions
Dress code: casual
Price range: $3-8

Rouladen

8   thin slices of inside round beef
8   strips of bacon
2   small onions quartered
2   cups water
    Dijon mustard

Dab one side of each inside round with mustard. Lay 1 slice of bacon on top and ¼ onion. Roll and pierce with a toothpick. Brown on all sides with oil. Add 2 cups water and simmer with lid on pot until tender (approx. 1 hour). Thicken with a paste of cornstarch and water to make a gravy.

Hint: to enrich flavour add beef cubes or Maggi seasoning, extra pepper, salt and onions. Serve with potatoes of choice, knoedel (dumplings) or egg noodles.
Serves 4

Erwtwensoep
(Dutch Pea Soup)

1 lb   split peas
3-4   litres of water
3-4   leeks
3   celery stalks (or cubed celeriac if available)
1   smoked pork hock
500g smoked sausages

Boil peas and pork hock together with water until peas are pureed (about 2½ hours). Add the vegetables for the last hour and the sausages for the last half hour. When all is done, cut up the pork hock meat into bite-sized pieces and add to soup. Stir and thicken if necessary with paste of flour and cold water. Season to taste with salt and pepper.
Serves 6-8

Grandview Inn

RR 4, Huntsville, Ont., P0A 1K0
(705) 789-4417

Manager: Randy Cooper
Chef: Randy Spencer

Grandview is "the luxury resort with a country-inn feeling" overlooking scenic Fairy Lake. Before the turn of the century, the original Grandview Farm began catering to summer tourists who arrived by steamer. Today, Grandview offers a number of dining options that are year round. The Inn Dining Room provides, beautiful decor and attentive service in a setting reminiscent of a country inn. Fall and winter offers a pub luncheon in the Owl's Nest and the summertime crowd can enjoy the casual lakeside setting of the Dockside Restaurant.

Reservations recommended
Season: year round
Type of cuisine: Continental
Licensed LLBO
Credit cards: Visa, AMEX, MC, En Route
No wheelchair access
Children's portions
Dress code: smart casual
Price range: $30-40

Traditional Onion Pudding Angela

1	loaf of stale homemade bread
6	large eggs
1 ¼ cups	milk
1 ¼ cups	chopped cooking onions
1 tsp	freshly chopped thyme
¼ tsp	freshly chopped rosemary
⅛ tsp	freshly cracked black pepper
½ tsp	white sugar
¼ cup	clarified butter

Tear loaf of bread into several pieces and soak in cold water for 10 seconds. Squeeze as much water as possible from the bread. In a large bowl, mix the first 8 ingredients, blend well. Coat the bottom and sides of a 12" deep dish pie plate with half the butter. Pour in the mixture and smooth out the top. Pour on remaining butter and bake at 375⁰ F till golden brown top and bottom (appoximately 45 minutes). Serve with roast beef or pork, smother with drippings and enjoy!

Serves 6-8

Canadian Pacific ■◢ Hotels & Resorts

Deerhurst Resort

RR 4, Huntsville, Ont., P0A 1K0
(705) 789-6411

Manager: Brian Lilley
Chef: Roger Tremblay

Originally built in 1896 as the first summer resort in the Huntsville area, Deerhurst Resort has grown over the century to become Ontario's largest and most comprehensive resort. Hints of the original inn are still evident in the warm elegance of The Dining Room at The Lodge, where fine cuisine and attentive service set a standard of warm hospitality in Muskoka. From May through October, patrons also enjoy the casual atmosphere of "Steamers" restaurant, while "The Pub" offers light fare in a friendly setting.

Reservations recommended
Season: year round
Type of cuisine: International/Regional
Licensed LLBO
Credit cards: all major
Wheelchair access
Children's portions
Dress code: smart casual
Price range: $30-40

From the Deerhurst Resort kitchens, this delicate recipe can be used with any type of fish from the Muskoka lakes.

Pickerel Forestiere

4-8 oz	fillet of fresh Pickerel
1/2 cup	sliced button mushrooms
1/2 cup	sliced shiitake mushrooms
1/4 cup	butter
2 oz	dry white wine
1 oz	lemon juice
2	small French shallots, chopped finely

Brown the pickerel in a frying pan with half of the butter, then place in oven at 350⁰ F for 10 minutes. Saute shallots and mushrooms. Add white wine and bring to a boil until the mixture reduces to half. Add lemon juice and stir. Remove from heat and mix in remainder of butter using a whisk. Remove pickerel from oven and pour finished sauce over fish and serve.

Preparation takes about 20 minutes, cooking about 20-30 minutes.

Serves 4-6

Cedar Grove
LODGE

P.O. Box 996 Huntsville, Ont., P0A 1K0
(705) 789-4036
1-800-461-4269

Since the 1930's the Fleming family have owned and operated this picturesque inn on beautiful Peninsula Lake in the area of the old settlement of Grassmere. Hearty home cooked meals are their specialty, and they offer a relaxed atmosphere for family reunions, meetings, conferences or a simple dinner for two. Docking is available for visiting boaters and lakeside log cabins with fireplaces house resort guests. Their meals have been a Muskoka tradition for many generations of visitors and local people alike.

Reservations accepted
Season: year round
Type of cuisine: Canadian
Not licensed
Credit cards: all major
No wheelchair access
Children's portions
Dress code: casual
Price range: $10-20

Beef Stir Fry

2 ¹/₂ lbs	round steak
¹/₄ cup	of water
⁵/₈ cup	soy sauce
¹/₂ cup	red wine
¹/₄ cup	honey
¹/₈ cup	cornstarch
¹/₂ cup	cooking oil
1 ¹/₂ cups	green onion-bias sliced in 2 inch lengths
1 ¹/₂ cups	sliced fresh mushrooms
1 cup	water chestnuts

Partially freeze the meat; slice thinly across the grain into bite-sized strips. Place in medium bowl. For marinade, combine water, soy sauce, wine, honey and cornstarch. Pour marinade over beef. Marinate for 30 minutes, stirring occasionally. Drain meat well, reserving the marinade.

Preheat a large skillet over high heat. Add oil, green onion, mushroom and water chestnuts. Stir-fry 2 minutes or until partially cooked. Remove onions, mushrooms and chestnuts. Stir-fry meat strips. Cook marinade until thickened and bubbly. Add to meat and vegetables and stir to coat. Cover and cook until heated through. Serve over hot cooked rice.

Serves 8

Area 3
Lake of Bays, Haliburton

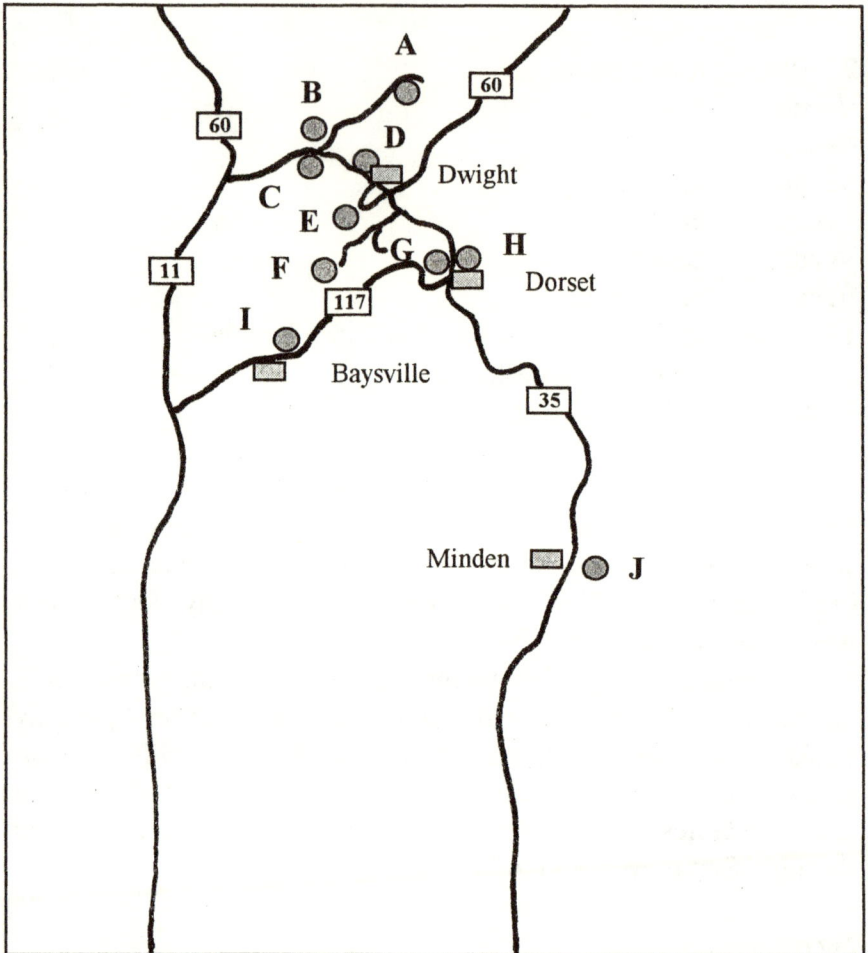

A

B

60

60

D

Dwight

C

E

G   H

F

Dorset

I

117

Baysville

11

35

Minden   J

Index

A- Ox-Bow Lodge

B- The Norsemen Restaurant

C- Joanne's Catering

D- Navigation Co. Depot

E- Nor ' Loch Lodge

F- Port Cunnington

G- Tom Salmon Inn

H- Cedar Narrows Restaurant

I- Country Kitchen

J- Austrian Village

The Portage Flyer, successor to the stage coach ran between Peninsula Lake and Lake of Bays, c. 1940.

General Information

<u>Waterways:</u> Lake of Bays, Ox-Bow Lake, Walker Lake, Gull River, Kawagama Lake, Kashagawigamog Lake

<u>Major Centres:</u> Baysville, Dorset, Dwight, Minden, Haliburton

<u>Cultural Attractions:</u> Lake of Bays: Baysville Arts & Crafts Show Haliburton: Highland Games, Haliburton Highland Museum, Rail's End Gallery

Ox-Bow Lodge

Limberlost Rd 8
RR 4, GRP Box 201, Huntsville, Ont., P0A 1K0
(705) 635-2514
1-800-461-4302

Owners: Jamie & Jill Wilson and Dave & Diane Dearlove
Chef: Alice Maxwell

Ox-Bow Lodge is known for its natural tranquil surroundings and beautiful scenery, not to mention the delicious, bountiful meals served up in home-cooked tradition with a gourmet flair.

The lodge originated in the early 1900's when the existing farm was expanded to a fishing camp. Today, in a modernized resort setting, Ox-Bow Lodge caters to individuals and families wanting to escape the city stress. Unwind in their private log cabins with fireplaces. Weddings, meetings and special functions are also carefully attended to.

Reservations accepted
Season: year round
Type of cuisine: Canadian
Licensed LLBO
Credit cards: Visa, Diners, MC
No wheelchair access
Children's portions
Dress code: casual
Price range: $10-15

Ox-Bow Lodge's Five Layer Blueberry Tart

Layer 1

2 cups   graham cracker crumbs
$^1/_2$ cup   melted butter

Blend together and press into a 9 x 13" pan. Bake 15 minutes at 300° F, then cool.

Layer 2
$^1/_2$ cup   soft butter creamed
$1^1/_2$ cups   icing sugar
2   eggs

Cream icing sugar and butter; beat in eggs until light. Spread over first layer.

Layer 3

Spread 1-19 oz can blueberry pie filling over layer 2.

Layer 4

1-19 oz   can crushed pineapple
1 cup   Cool Whip

Fold together and spread over layer 3.

Layer 5

Sprinkle $^1/_2$ cup of graham crumbs over entire top of layer 4 and garnish top with fresh Muskoka wild blueberries. Let entire dessert stand overnight. Enjoy!

Serves 16

The Norsemen Restaurant
RR 4, Huntsville, Ont., P0A 1K0
(705) 635-2473

Owners: Enno and Lynda Kerckhoff
Chef: Raymond McGuire

Established as a homestead in the late 1870's by the Walker family, "Muskoka's best kept secret" was known as the Royal Oak Lodge and Walker Lake Resort before being transformed into its present rustic elegance as a last reminder of Muskoka's famous and gracious resort and dining heritage.

Lynda and Enno have enhanced the tradition of truly exceptional dining and warm hospitality. The combination of extraordinary cuisine in a natural Muskoka setting, minutes from Huntsville and major resorts, make the Norsemen a precious secret to discover. Accomodation in well-appointed cottages is also available.

Reservations accepted
Season: Year round-Winter: Thurs to Sun
Type of cuisine: Canadian/European
Licensed LLBO
Credit cards: Visa, MC
No wheelchair access
Children's portions
Dress code: casual
Price range: $30-40

The Norsemen proudly presents a delicious recipe featuring Chef Raymond McGuire's own vinaigrette salad dressings, made right on the premises... and sold locally!

Chef Raymond's Chicken Breast Supreme BBQ with Fruit Vinaigrette

2	medium chicken breasts, with skin removed
1	bottle (375 ml) of Chef Raymond's fruit vinaigrette (your favourite choice)
¼ cup	berries-suggest same as vinaigrette
1tsp	cornstarch

Marinate chicken in Chef Raymond's fruit vinaigrette for 24 hours (keep refrigerated). Remove chicken from marinade and barbeque until done. Take care not to over-cook or some flavour will be lost. Skim the oil off the remaining marinade and bring to a boil. Add the ¼ cup of berries and simmer for 2-3 minutes. Mix 2 tsps. of water with about 1 tsp. of cornstarch and add to hot berry dressing. Stir constantly for about 2 minutes and pour small amount onto cooked chicken breasts.

Serves 2

Joanne's Catering

RR 4, Huntsville, Ont., P0A 1K0
(705) 635-1466

Owner: Joanne Cunnington
Chef: Joanne Cunnington

Dining el fresco? Cottagers, boaters, visitors and local residents can all enjoy the culinary delights of Joanne's kitchen. Having grown up in the resort business, Joanne has been catering for all occasions, indoors or outdoors, since 1984. For easy entertainment, treat your holiday guests to special menu items. Delivery and in-home catering are also available. Please call Joanne for complete details.

Season: year round
Type of cuisine: Canadian/Specialty
Prices: available on request

Cream of Celery Soup

1/2 cup	butter, melted
1 cup	rice flour
2 1/2 cups	diced celery & water (boil until tender)
8 cups	milk
1 1/2 tsp	salt
1/4 tsp	celery salt
1/4 tsp	seasoned salt
1/8 tsp	cayenne pepper
1 tbsp	chicken soup base

Add flour to butter and mix until blended. Add liquids, seasonings and bring to boil. Stir constantly. Let boil for 7-10 minutes, until there is no taste of flour. Serve with celery leaf for garnish.

Serves 6

THE NAVIGATION CO. DEPOT

The Navigation Co. Depot
Hwy 60, (The edge of Dwight)
Huntsville, Ont., P0A 1K0
(705) 635-1515

Manager & Chef: Jeff Suddaby & Ron Gostlin

During the 1940's and 50's, the Huntsville Lake of Bays Navigation Co. provided transportation service for residents and tourists. 1989 saw the opening of the Navigation Co. Depot at the edge of Dwight. Named for the location of the company's first restaurant, "The Diner", which opened the previous year at the location of the original Navigation Co. headquarters, on Huntsville's town dock. In keeping with the spirit of the Transportation Co., the Depot lends its character to the feel of the rail services of the time and area. "The Portage Flyer", one of the shortest railways of all time, carried boats passengers between Peninsula Lake and Lake of Bays from North Portage and South Portage. The Depot's flair for Cajun and Mexican favourites, mixed with unique styles of service make for a memorable meal. "We take pride in our ribs that will melt in your mouth".

Reservations not needed   **No wheelchair access**
Season: year round   **Children's portions**
Type of cuisine: Canadian/Specialty   **Dress code:** casual
Licensed LLBO   **Price range:** $4-14
Credit cards: Visa, AMEX, MC

Deep Fried Ice Cream

1 part ground cinnamon
10 parts sugar
ice cream
Wayne Gretzky cereal
honey or maple syrup
whipped cream
blanched almonds
fresh strawberries

Mix the sugar and cinnamon in a flat pan or tray. Form the ice cream into balls approximately 2 1/2". Roll the ice cream balls in the cinnamon sugar mix. After coating, place in a bowl of Wayne Gretzky cereal that has been crushed. Pack the dry cereal onto the outside of the ice cream.

Place in the freezer until solid. Remove from the freezer and immediately place into the deep fryer at 350^0 F for approximately 9 seconds. Place in a serving bowl. Add honey or maple syrup to taste. Top with whipped cream, blanched almonds and a strawberry.

Nor ' Loch Lodge & Resort

Dwight, Ont., P0A 1H0
(705) 635-2231
1-800-565-2231 (in Ontario)

Your hosts: Gary and Margaret Hanel & John and Karen Szykoluk
Chef: Larry Vale

Originally built at the turn of the century, this lakeside resort, nestled in tall pines, is only 15 minutes from Algonquin Park. The pastoral setting offers scenic views of the sparkling waters of the Lake of Bays. Docking is available on site from spring through the summer.

Enjoy fine dining in a relaxed atmosphere featuring theme nights and Nor ' Loch's famous prime rib buffet. Excellent group facilities are available as well as well-appointed accomodation units.

Reservations recommended
Season: year round
Type of cuisine: Canadian/Continental
Licensed LLBO
Credit cards: Visa, MC
No wheelchair access
Children's portions
Dress code: casual
Price range: $12-20

Nor ' Loch's Own Wild Rice Pancakes

2	eggs
2 2/3 cups	buttermilk
2 tbsp	butter, melted
2 cups	unbleached all purpose flour
2 tbsp	granulated sugar
2 tsp	baking powder
3/4 tsp	salt
1/2 tsp	baking soda
1 cup	cooked wild rice

In a large bowl whisk together the eggs, buttermilk and melted butter. Stir together the flour, sugar, baking powder, salt and soda. Sprinkle the dry ingredients, then the rice, evenly over the buttermilk batter. Stir together with a fork, just mixing enough to blend wet and dry together. Heat griddle to medium high, pour 1/4 cup at a time. Fry till golden. Serve with blueberry sauce or maple syrup.

Makes 16-4" pancakes

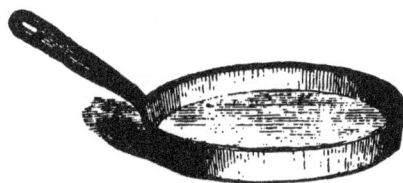

Port Cunnington Lodge
RR 1, Dwight, Ont., P0A 1H0
Lake of Bays
(705) 635-2505

Your host: Audrey Loader

    In 1890, the original Cunnington homestead became Port Cunnington Lodge and was been family operated for quite some time. In this secluded resort on Lake of Bays there are only two things that matter-the weather and what's for dinner. If the tranquil setting alone is not enough to entice you, the fine cuisine certainly will.

Reservations recommended
Season: year round
Type of cuisine: Canadian
Licensed LLBO
Credit cards: Visa, AMEX, MC
No wheelchair access
Children's portions
Dress code: casual
Price range: $10-20

This recipe was named after the maple trees at Point Ideal that supply the area with a plentiful amount of rich maple syrup each season

Point Ideal Maple Syrup Pie

1 can	Eagle Brand condensed milk
2/3 cup	pure maple syrup
1 pinch	salt
1	baked pie shell
	whipped cream
	chopped/pieces walnuts

In a medium saucepan combine the maple syrup, condensed milk and salt. Cook over low heat stirring constantly, to avoid scorching, until the mixture bubbles. Cook for 4 minutes, until the filling is thickened. Pour into baked pie shell. Let cool completely, about 2-3 hours. Before serving, top with whipped cream. Sprinkle with chopped walnuts or walnut pieces.

Serves many

DORSET, ONTARIO

The Tom Salmon Inn

3 Main St., Dorset, Ont., P0A 1E0
(705) 766-2261

Owners: Cam Norton & Sam Ion
Chef: Ryan Trudeau

Who's the old guy on the sign? He was the son of Col. Salmon, an officer of the 57th Bengal Native Infantry in India, grandson of a Lord Mayor of London, husband of Elizabeth Robson, life-long friend of Rudyard Kipling, adventurer, and my great grandfather. He arrived on the Lake of Bays in 1870, lived with the natives, settled long enough in Dorset to rename it after his home in Dorsetshire, England. We have it on good authority that the tourtiere recipe we are using at the Inn comes from the kitchen of Canada's Prime Ministers, first appearing on John Diefenbaker's table. Enjoy!

- Sam Ion

Reservations not necessary
Season: year round; winter closed Wed & Thurs
Type of cuisine: Canadian/Italian
Licensed LLBO
Credit cards: Visa, MC
No wheelchair access
Children's portions
Dress code: casual
Price range: $5-15

Tourtiere

1 ½ lbs	lean minced pork
½ lb	minced beef
1	clove garlic, crushed
1 ½ tsp	salt
½ tsp	thyme
½ tsp	sage
½ tsp	dry mustard
⅛ tsp	cloves
1 can	consomme, undiluted
1	large cooked potato, mashed

Mix first 9 ingredients together in a pan. Bring to a boil. Simmer, uncovered, for 30 minutes. Add the mashed potato.

Pastry

4 cups	sifted all purpose flour
1 1/2 tsp	salt
1 cup	lard
1 tbsp	hard butter
2	beaten eggs
6 tbsp	cold water

Sift flour and salt into a bowl. Cut in lard until mixture resembles fine oatmeal, then cut in hard butter coarsely. Stir in eggs and water mixed together. Chill dough for 30 minutes before rolling out. Line 2, 9" pans with pastry. Add meat mixture. Dampen rims and roll out top crusts. Seal edges. Bake at 425^0 F for 15 minutes. Reduce heat to 350^0 F. Continue baking for 25-30 minutes.

Serves 12-14

Cedar Narrows Restaurant & Dining Lounge
Dorset, Ont., P0A 1E0
(705) 766-2344

Your hosts: Janine & Neil Scott

In 1871, you would have arrived in Dorset on the Iroquois steamer across the road from their present site. Today you may dock your boat at the lakeside patio and enjoy a light meal overlooking the Narrows. Or, you may dine in a relaxed atmosphere reminiscent of past lumbering days. Choose from a wide selection of fine foods and wines served by the warm and friendly staff. Unwind at the end of the day in their comfortable lounge.

Reservations recommended
Season: year round; winter: Wed. to Sun.
Type of cuisine: Canadian
Licensed LLBO
Credit cards: Visa, AMEX, MC
No wheelchair access
Children's portions
Dress code: casual
Price range: $7-20

Chocolate Pecan Pie

1 cup	corn syrup
2 cups	honey
1/2 lb	butter (soft)
6	whole eggs
2	brown sugar
1/4 cup	grated semi sweet chocolate
2 cups	pecans (whole)
9 "	unbaked pie shell

Combine eggs, sugar, honey and corn syrup. Melt butter and fold into honey mixture. Add pecans. Pour into pie shell. Top with chocolate. Bake at 325^0 F for 25 to 30 minutes, or until set.

Serves many

The Country Kitchen Restaurant
Birch Glen Resort,
Baysville, Ont., P0B 1A0
(705) 767-3175

Manager: Penny Hube
Chef: Wes Edwards

This restaurant is situated at Birch Glen Resort on beautiful Lake of Bays. Nestled among the pine and birch trees, the restaurant was established by Dr. Black and his family, who were from Bracebridge. Now open to the public, as well as resort guests, Penny and Wes invite you to discover the "rustic elegance" of the dining room. Docking facilities are also available.

Reservations accepted
Season: year round
Type of cuisine: Canadian
Licensed LLBO
Credit cards: Visa, MC
Wheelchair access
Children's portions
Dress code: casual
Price range: $13-18

Pork Tenderloin with French Mustard and Bread & Butter Pickles

8	pieces pork tenderloin (3-4 oz each)
	bread & butter pickles in juice
1 tbsp	french mustard
1/4 cup	white wine
1/4 cup	finely minced onions
1/2 cup	whipping cream
1 tsp	vegetable oil

Flatten pork tenderloin pieces to approximately 1/4" thickness. Sear pork in a frying pan on high heat. Cover, reduce heat and cook until done. Remove from pan. Add oil and saute onions over moderately high heat. Deglaze pan with white wine. Add mustard, cream and 1 tbsp pickle juice. Replace tenderloin in pan, and cook over low heat until sauce is reduced by half. Garnish with bread and butter pickles.

This dish is excellent with either potatoes or rice and your favourite steamed vegetables!

Serves 4

Austrian Village Restaurant

Austrian Village Restaurant
South Lake Road
Minden, Ont., K0M 2K0
(705) 286-1081

Your hosts (and chefs): Margaret & Ludwig Pilz

For 16 years the Austrian Village has been offering European style dining and atmosphere in the Minden area. Situated on an 18 acre wooded property, it boasts a swimming pool, an outdoor patio and a biergarten for the summer months. The Pilz's also offer a convenient bed and breakfast service for their guests.

Reservations accepted
Season: year round
Type of cuisine: Canadian/European
Licensed LLBO
Credit cards: Visa, MC
No wheelchair access
Children's portions
Dress code: casual
Price range: $10-13

Wiener Schnitzel

5 oz	veal schnitzel-not too thin
1	egg (beaten)
1/2 cup	milk
	flour for dipping
	bread crumbs for coating
1	slice of lemon

Pound veal on both sides. Dip veal in flour. Blend egg and milk. Dip veal in egg mixture. Coat veal well with bread crumbs, pressing crumbs into meat. Brown coated veal in hot oil on both sides. Serve hot with lemon slice, brown rice or home fries.

Area 4
Algonquin, Oxtongue

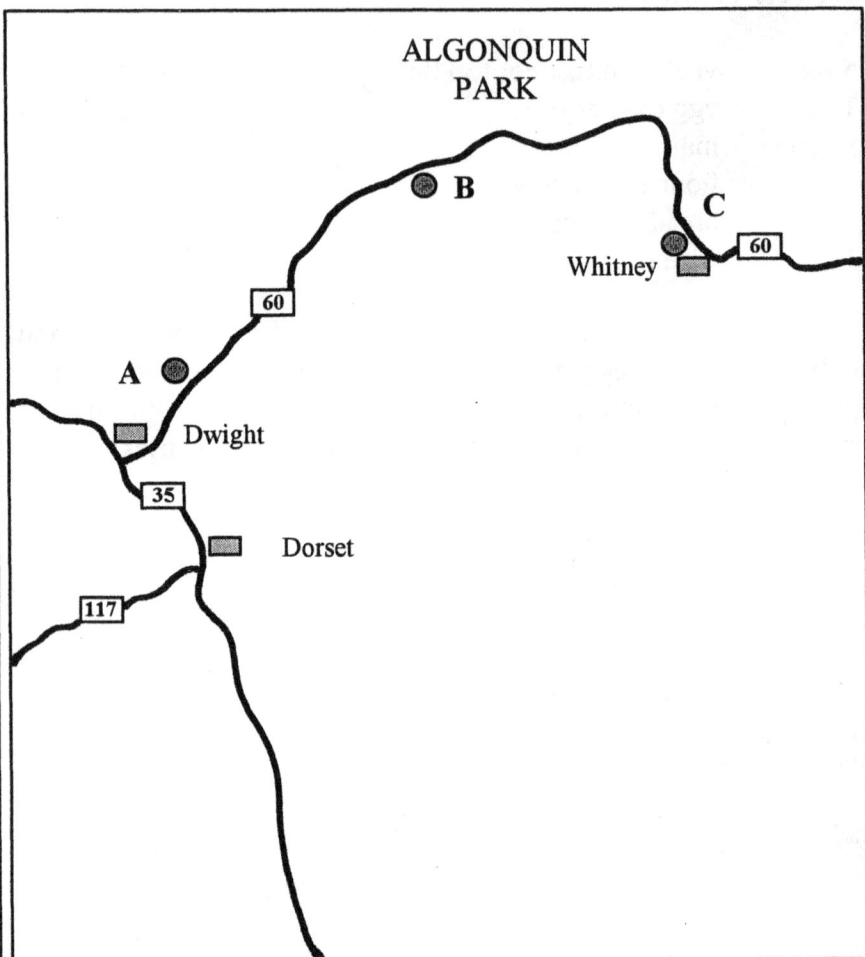

ALGONQUIN
PARK

B

C

60

Whitney

60

A

Dwight

35

Dorset

117

Index

A- Paddle Inn Restaurant
B- Killarney Lodge
C- Bear Trail Inn

Nominigan Lodge, Algonquin Park, c. 1933.

Nominigan Lodge, Algonquin Park, c. 1933.

General Information

Waterways: Joe Lake, Lake of Two Rivers, Oxtongue Lake, Galeairy Lake

Major Centres: Algonquin Park, Oxtonque Lake Area, Whitney

Cultural Attractions: Pioneer Logging Museum, Algonquin Park Museum

Paddle Inn Restaurant/Timber Trail Algonquin

RR 1 Dwight,
Oxtongue Lake
(705) 635-1097
1-800-463-2995

Owner/Chef: Sandra Rae

Paddle Inn Restaurant at Timber Trail Algonquin is definitely a family affair! While the kids feed the chipmunks and enjoy the playground, we suggest you linger over our delicious homemade desserts and coffee. It's a short paddle from Ragged Falls. Yes! People do paddle in to enjoy our homemade meals and personal service. Enjoy our patio in the summer time.

Reservations not required
Season: year round
Type of cuisine: Canadian/European
Not licensed
Credit cards: Visa
No wheelchair access
Children's portions
Dress code: casual
Price range: $3-8

Warm Chicken Salad with Basil Dressing

1¹/₂ cups	washed, dried, chopped salad greens (lettuce, tomato, green peppers, etc)
	basil dressing (see below)
1	4oz boneless, cubed chicken breast
¹/₄ cup	sliced mushrooms
3 tbsp	peanut oil
2 tbsp	white wine
	pinch of thyme, rosemary, salt

Put salad greens in a glass bowl. Sprinkle on small amount of Basil dressing (or any oil & vinegar dressing). Heat oil in wok over high heat until oil smokes. Stir fry chicken and mushrooms in wok until chicken is no longer pink (about 2 minutes). Add spices, salt and white wine. Pour over greens and serve immediately.

Serves 1

Paddle Inn Basil Dressing

³/₄ cup	peanut oil
¹/₄ cup	white vinegar
10	fresh basil leaves
¹/₄ tsp	pepper
¹/₄ tsp	celery salt

Blend together in blender. Store unused portion in refrigerator.

Makes 1 cup

Killarney Lodge

Algonquin Park, Ont., P0A 1K0
(705) 633-5551 (May-October)

Your hosts: Linda and Eric Miglin

Have you heard the wild Timber Wolves in Algonquin Park? Or seen moose, white tailed deer or taken an evening walk with Park naturalists? Killarney Lodge is located at the heart of Algonquin Park.

Built of native white pine in 1935, the intimate log dining room boasts a country inn atmosphere of quiet charm and hearty homemade cuisine. Roasts, fresh vegetables, fruit pies and homemade rolls are baked right on the premises.

Reservations accepted
Season: May-October
Type of cuisine: Canadian
Not licensed
Credit cards: Visa, MC
No wheelchair access
Children's portions
Dress code: smart casual
Price range: $25-35

Chunky Carrot Soup

6 tbsp	butter
1	medium-size spanish onion
3	cloves garlic, minced
1/3	cup finely chopped ginger
8	cups chicken stock
1 1/2	pounds carrots, peeled and cut into 1/2 in. pieces
1	cup dry white wine
1 tbsp	lemon juice
	freshly chopped chives

Melt the butter in a large stock pot over medium heat. Add the onion, ginger and garlic and saute for 10 minutes, or until tender. Add the stock, carrots and wine. Heat to boiling. Reduce heat and simmer over medium heat until the carrots are tender which should be about 40 minutes. Reserve 1/3 of the above mixture in a separate pot. Puree the remaining soup in a food processor until a smooth consistency is obtained. Add the puree mixture to the reserved soup, as set aside before. Season with lemon juice and salt and pepper to taste. Sprinkle with freshly chopped chives.

Serves 6

Bear Trail Inn Resort

Whitney, Ont., K0J 2M0
(613) 637-2662

Manager: John Sorenson
Chef: Pat Cybulski

Bear Trail Inn Resort is a quiet luxury resort on the shores of Lake Galeairy, a great swimming lake shared with Algonquin Park. Algonquin Park, the oldest park in Ontario, offers a new Pioneer Logging Exhibit (a short 5 minute drive), and a 90% chance of spotting one of 4000 moose in the wilderness. Mountain bike and hiking trails, outdoor pool, hot tub, jacuzzi suites and romantic log cabins are ideal for couples. "Let us pamper you".

Reservations accepted
Season: year round
Type of cuisine: Canadian/European
Licensed LLBO
Credit cards: Visa, MC, Diner's Club
No wheelchair access
No children's portions
Dress code: smart casual
Price range: $22-28

Danish Duck

1	whole duck, eviscerated
4 cups	cold water
2	apples, peeled and diced
10	pitted prunes
4	bacon strips

Place innards of duck in pot. Add cold water and simmer for 1 hour. The broth will be used later for gravy.

Clean cavity of duck and sprinkle with salt. Fill with prunes and apples. Place bacon on top of duck, add 1/2 cup of water to pan and cook for 30 minutes at 350° F or until done. Skin should be crisp. Discard drippings from pan. Quarter duck to make 4 portions.

Gravy

Use stock and add 1 tbsp gravy base with 2 tbsp cornstarch with cold water and add to boiling stock. Add 1/4 cup white wine. Simmer till thick.

Serve with Danish sweet potatoes and red cabbage.

Serves 4

INDEX OF ESTABLISHMENTS

H.M.S. Segwun 18
Sherwood Inn (Poached Pears Filled with Smoked Duck
  and Saffron Rice) 6
Sloan's Restaurant and Tavern (Steak Neptune) 16

The Tom Salmon Inn (Tourtiere) 54
Touch of Class 30

INDEX OF RECIPES

Desserts

Chocolate Pecan Pie (Cedar Narrows Restaurant
  and Dining Lounge)   57
Deep-Fried Ice Cream (The Navigation Co.
  Depot)   49
Five Layer Blueberry Tart (Ox-bow Lodge)   43
Gratinated Fruit Dessert (Muskoka Sands)   15
Point Ideal Maple Syrup Pie (Port Cunnington
  Lodge)   53
Zabaglione (Gryffin Lodge)   25

Miscellaneous

Hot Spiced Wassail (Muskoka Pioneer Village)   27
Traditional Onion Pudding Angela (Grandview
  Inn)   35
Wild Rice Pancakes (Nor'Loch Lodge)   51